TEEN LIFE™

FREQUENTLY ASKED QUESTIONS ABOUT

Plagiarism

Liz
Sonneborn

ROSEN
PUBLISHING®

New York

Published in 2011 by The Rosen Publishing Group, Inc.
29 East 21st Street, New York, NY 10010

Library of Congress Cataloging-in-Publication Data

Sonneborn, Liz.
Frequently asked questions about plagiarism / Liz Sonneborn.—
1st ed.
     p. cm.—(FAQ: teen life)
Includes bibliographical references and index.
ISBN 978-1-4488-1330-8 (lib. bdg.)
1. Plagiarism—Juvenile literature. I. Title.
PN167.S66 2011
808—dc22

                                        2010016340

Manufactured in the United States of America

CPSIA Compliance Information: Batch #W11YA: For further information, contact Rosen Publishing, New York,
New York, at 1-800-237-9932.

CONTENTS

one

WHAT IS PLAGIARISM?

In late April 2006, nineteen-year-old Kaavya Viswanathan was on top of the world. She was a sophomore at Harvard University, arguably the most prestigious school of higher learning in the United States. Even better, she had just become a published novelist. Two years earlier, she had scored a two-book contract with Little, Brown. The publisher had high hopes for Viswanathan and her first book, *How Opal Mehta Got Kissed, Got Wild, and Got a Life*. In fact, everyone she met thought this attractive, talented young woman was only beginning what was bound to be a fabulous career as a writer.

Just when it seemed Viswanathan's life couldn't get any better, everything came crashing down. Harvard's student newspaper, the *Harvard Crimson*, published an article that alleged she had stolen thirteen passages in her book, almost word for word, from another novelist named

Nineteen-year-old writer Kaavya Viswanathan lost her book contract when it was reported that she had plagiarized passages of her first novel.

Megan McCafferty. Viswanathan's troubles didn't end there. Other reporters began taking a close look at her book. They found she had also borrowed the words of several other writers, including Sophie Kinsella, Meg Cabot, and Salman Rushdie.

Viswanathan frantically tried to explain what had happened. Appearing on NBC's *Today* show, she claimed that it was all a big accident. She said she had a photographic memory. After reading the other authors' works, she had unknowingly memorized them and, forgetting their sources, thought she had come up with the stolen passages herself. Viswanathan's explanation did little to repair her tattered reputation. Journalists and critics condemned what she had done, and her publisher recalled her book and canceled her contract. In a flash, it looked as though Kaavya Viswanathan's brilliant literary career was over.

Copying and Copyright

Just what had Viswanathan done that was so bad that so many people thought she deserved to be humiliated and punished? In short, she had plagiarized. She had taken the work of other people and claimed it as her own.

The allegations leveled at Viswanathan put her in good company. Plenty of famous people have been accused of plagiarism. They include the great novelist Vladimir Nabokov, the esteemed historian Stephen Ambrose, and the former Russian president Vladimir Putin. Even civil rights hero Martin Luther King Jr. has been called a plagiarist.

In those cases, the people who supposedly plagiarized stole someone else's words. But other creative works can be plagiarized, too. For instance, plagiarists often try to pass off another person's artwork, music, or data as their own. Even ideas can be plagiarized.

Is plagiarizing a crime? Not always, but it can be. Books, newspaper and magazine articles, paintings, photographs, films, videos, and all sorts of other media are often protected by copyright. A copyright means that no one else can use the work without permission from the copyright holder. (Usually, the person who created the work owns the copyright.) Anyone who

On its Web site (http://copyright.gov), the U.S. Copyright Office provides the public with information about what a copyright is and how to register for one.

copies from a work under copyright without permission is committing copyright infringement. That *is* a crime, and the copyright holder can take the offender to court. It's not easy to win a copyright infringement case, though. Copyright holders usually have to prove that the plagiarizer kept them from making money they otherwise would have earned from their work.

Is it always illegal to copy from a copyrighted work? In a word, no. Anyone can reproduce a portion of a copyrighted work under what is called fair use. Figuring out exactly what is fair use is very tricky, though. In general, fair use allows you to quote a little bit of a long work. For instance, one sentence quoted out of a five-hundred-page book is likely going to fall under fair use. Short works, like song lyrics, are another matter, however. Say a song has twenty lines of lyrics. If someone publishes ten lines in a book without permission, that person can be accused of copyright infringement.

Works that were once under copyright can also lose their protection. They are then in the public domain. If a work is in the public domain, anyone anywhere can do with it whatever he or she wants. But keep in mind that even if something is in the public domain, if you copy from it, you are still plagiarizing. For instance, let's say you're taking a creative writing course, and you turn in a few chapters from F. Scott Fitzgerald's *The Great Gatsby* as your own work. The novel is in the public domain, so you haven't broken any laws. But your teacher won't appreciate what you've done. She'll still say that you plagiarized and probably will give you an F for your efforts.

Types of Plagiarizing

Like that latter example, some types of plagiarism are very easy to recognize. Think of a guy who buys a research paper about Emily Dickinson's poetry and turns it in to his American literature teacher with his name on it. Or think of a girl who pads her portfolio with photographs taken by her best friend and hopes her art teacher can't tell. But sometimes just what constitutes plagiarism isn't so clear-cut. It is in those instances that otherwise honest students are most likely to get themselves into trouble.

One kind of accidental plagiarism is what Kaavya Viswanathan said she did. It's called cryptomnesia. Some psychologists believe that people caught up in making a creative work can lose sight of the source of their ideas. They might honestly think they came up with a certain notion, out of the blue, when, in fact, it was something they had read or heard before. Experts, though, doubt that people are likely to reproduce complete paragraphs, word for word, in this kind of unconscious way. In other words, if you are accused of copying entire passages from a source, don't expect a cryptomnesia defense to get you very far.

Another type of plagiarizing is cutting and pasting. Suppose you are assigned a paper on the Boston Massacre. Online you find a great article on the topic in a military history magazine. You copy and paste the article, and switch a few words around to make it more your own. You feel great. In record time, you've completed your assignment, and it's really well-written. There's one problem, though. Your paper is plagiarized. Just changing a few words doesn't alter the fact that you're taking someone else's work and calling it your own.

OK, you want to start over. This time, you'll rewrite the article, reworking each and every sentence. What you're trying to do is paraphrase—putting another person's ideas in your own words. But if you stick to the original article's structure, laboriously rewriting each sentence and paragraph, you are still plagiarizing. Essentially, you've just reproduced the ideas and structure of the article, without adding any of your own ideas to the mix.

Avoiding plagiarism is not as simple as it might seem. Students need to not only know exactly what plagiarism is but also work on developing skills, such as note taking, paraphrasing, quoting, and citing sources.

With all that in mind, you're ready to take another shot. This time, you are more careful in your paraphrasing, you rework the structure of the article, and you insert some original ideas into your paper. Even with all that work, you still may be accused of plagiarism. In most assignments, especially in research papers, you are expected to make it clear what ideas are your own and what ideas are someone else's. Remember that plagiarism is not just stealing someone's words. It is also stealing his or her ideas. If you use another person's ideas, you have to make that clear in your text with citations, *and* you have to provide information about where the reader can find those sources with a bibliography. (For more detailed information about citations and bibliographies, see chapter 3.)

So now you know something about what plagiarizing is. A cut-and-paste job with a few word changes is plagiarism. A clumsy paraphrase that adds nothing new is plagiarism. A mixture of your ideas and others' ideas without properly noting which is which is plagiarism. You probably also realize that avoiding plagiarism is harder than you may have thought. But that leaves another important question still unanswered: why should you care about plagiarism in the first place?

Myths and Facts

Plagiarism is on the rise.

Fact ➔ It's common to see television news reports and newspaper headlines declaring that plagiarism is an "epidemic" among today's students. In fact, scholars disagree about whether students plagiarize more now than they did in the past. Some studies show an increase, but many do not. Plagiarism expert Donald McCabe, however, has suggested that even if the absolute level of plagiarism hasn't changed, in recent years cutting and pasting has become much more common. Speaking on National Public Radio, he explained, "I think what's different now is that the Internet provides such a vast resource that's so easily accessible, that those students who are engaging in cut-and-paste plagiarism are doing it a lot more often, and I think that's where the explosion is."

It's impossible to plagiarize your own work.

Fact ➔ Many students assume that there's nothing wrong with turning the same paper into two different teachers as long as the work is their own. In fact, they are committing self-plagiarism. When teachers assign papers, they are assuming that the work you turn in is unique. Therefore, if you recycle one of your old papers, you are as guilty of plagiarism as you would be if you submitted a paper written by someone else. If you are assigned a paper related to a topic you've already written about, you may be able to reuse some of your research, however. Just be sure to check with your teacher to make sure that's allowed.

Every high school student plagiarizes.

Fact ➡ Even if you know a lot of students who have plagiarized, don't make the mistake of thinking everyone does it. Statistics on the rate of plagiarism differ, but McCabe told the *Christian Science Monitor* in 2006 that, according to his well-respected research, 58 percent of high school students admitted to committing an act of plagiarism in the previous year. Of course, the actual rate is probably higher because some plagiarists may not have been willing to admit what they had done. Even so, McCabe's figure suggests that about four out of ten students in high school never resort to plagiarism to get a good grade.

two

WHY SHOULD YOU CARE ABOUT PLAGIARIZING?

So what's the big deal about plagiarism? Sure, it may bend your teacher out of shape, but in the real world, who really cares? After all, you're not Kaavya Viswanathan. If you screw up your term paper, no one's going to put you on national television to explain why. You're not some famous writer or musician who would disappoint legions of fans if you put your name on someone else's article or song. You're just some kid trying to get through English lit or world history with a decent grade. You're busy. You've only got so much time for class work. Does it really matter if you take a shortcut here and there? In other words, what's so wrong with plagiarizing? A good way to answer this question is to stop thinking of yourself as the plagiarizer, and instead imagine what it's like to be a victim of plagiarism. Here's a mental

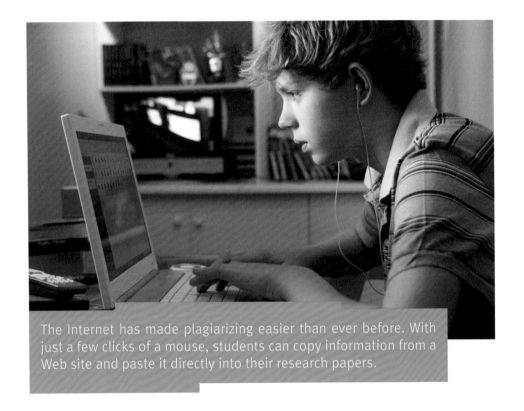

The Internet has made plagiarizing easier than ever before. With just a few clicks of a mouse, students can copy information from a Web site and paste it directly into their research papers.

exercise that might help you see how plagiarism looks from the other side.

Suppose you really love obscure Japanese anime. You decide to write your own blog about the subject. In your spare time, you start rewatching old favorites and seeking out new stuff. After each screening, you take notes. You also search the Web and visit the library, looking for any articles about the films you've watched. You take notes on these, too. You carefully start writing reviews in which you quote what other people have said about the films. Sometimes, you agree with them. Other times, you argue that their opinions are wrong.

With each review, you get more and more comments. Many of them compliment your reviews. Some disagree with them, but that's exciting, too. People are taking you and your ideas seriously. You have a loyal and growing readership that wants to hear what you have to say.

Three Blogs

One day, you're surfing the Web and discover another blog about anime. Well, it's not really another blog. It's an exact copy of yours except it has someone else's name at the top. There are no links to your blog, no citations that explain the material was written by you. Just like at your blog, readers are leaving positive comments, but they are praising the person who took your reviews, not you.

Imagine how you'd feel. You'd be furious, wouldn't you? Think of all the hard work you put into thinking about your reviews and trying to communicate your ideas. Now someone else just slaps up a blog and takes credit for everything you've done.

You keep surfing and, in no time, you find another blog that has borrowed your work. But instead of reproducing it exactly, about every other word has been replaced with a synonym of the original word. The changes make the writing sound strange and awkward. Not surprisingly, there aren't many comments praising the reviews.

How would you feel about this blogger? Sure, the plagiarist didn't copy your exact words without your permission, like the first blogger did. But wouldn't you still be angry? After all, you spent hours getting every essay just right, only to have someone come along and mess up your writing.

Now, on the same bad day, imagine you came across a third blog. Here again are all your reviews. Like the other two blogs, this one has someone else's name on it. But this time, every review is enclosed in quotation marks and ends with a link to your blog.

At least this blogger gave you credit, and the links might increase traffic to your blog. On the other hand, you notice that plenty of commenters didn't notice the links. Even with the citations, not all readers seem to realize the blogger lifted every-thing from your site. You may not be as mad at him as you are at the other bloggers. Still, you can't help but feel bothered by the whole thing. If the third blogger was interested enough in your work to link to it, why didn't he take the time to at least explain what he liked about your reviews?

The Plagiarist as Thief

The first blogger is an example of the worst kind of plagiarist. The guy is not only a thief but also a liar. He stole all your work and then lied by saying it was his. This is the kind of person you become when you copy down text word for word and try to pass it off as your own writing. It doesn't matter if it comes from a book, a Web site, or anywhere else. If you commit this type of plagiarism, you will be a thief and a liar, too.

What about the second blogger? He at least had the decency not to steal every word you wrote. But is what he did so much bet-ter? It's not as though he showed respect for your work. In fact, he

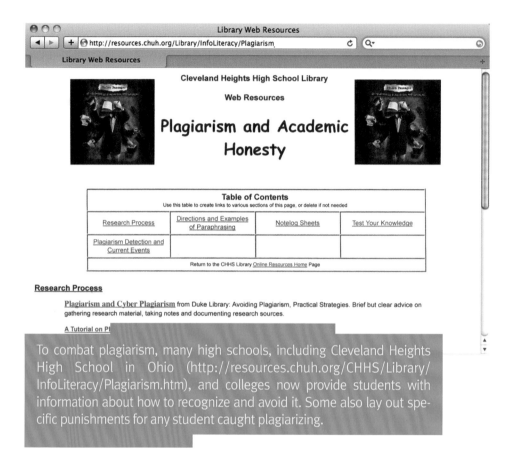

To combat plagiarism, many high schools, including Cleveland Heights High School in Ohio (http://resources.chuh.org/CHHS/Library/InfoLiteracy/Plagiarism.htm), and colleges now provide students with information about how to recognize and avoid it. Some also lay out specific punishments for any student caught plagiarizing.

didn't seem to hesitate to turn it into a garbled mush. If you "write" a paper by copying someone's work and changing a few words here and there, you are essentially acting just like this blogger. Even if you don't care about the original author's pride in his work, remember that this type of plagiarizing is easy to catch. If you turn in a paper with a bunch of strange word choices, your teacher won't have much trouble figuring out what you did.

The third blogger at least gave you credit, so it's not really plagiarism, is it? Well, yes, it is. The blogger was upfront about where he got his material, but he didn't write it. He's an honest thief, but he's still a thief.

Who Does Plagiarism Hurt?

Student plagiarists always have excuses for what they've done. "I ran out of time." "The assignment was stupid." "English isn't my first language." "My mom would kill me if I didn't get an A." "I'm a terrible writer." "I won't be able to get into the college I want to go to if I don't get really good grades."

There might be something to any of these excuses, although they probably won't get you off the hook. But saying that plagiarism doesn't hurt anyone won't cut it. When you take someone else's work, you are stealing from him or her. That's why lawyers call creative works intellectual property. In a way, copying another person's words or ideas isn't all that different from breaking into someone's house and making off with his or her flat-screen television. You are taking something that it not yours, and it's not right.

But the person you steal from is not the only one hurt by your plagiarism. You hurt your teacher, too. By plagiarizing, you are insulting your teacher's intelligence. In essence, you are saying your teacher is too stupid to figure out what you've done, which in most cases isn't even close to being true. You might not like your teachers, but underestimating their ability to sniff out plagiarism is a big mistake.

You also hurt your fellow students. Let's say you plagiarize a research paper and pull it off. Your teacher doesn't realize

Don't assume that your teachers won't notice your plagiarism. Most, especially those who have been on the job a few years, are experts at spotting copied work.

what you've done and gives you a good grade. You got what you wanted, but in the process you've made all the nonplagiarists in your class into suckers. Even though they worked hard and you barely did a thing, you might have made a better grade. In fact, because you plagiarized, your paper was probably more polished than many of your classmates'. The teacher might have graded their honest work lower because it paled in comparison with your dishonest work.

There is still one more person your plagiarism hurts—you. By not doing your own work, you miss the chance to learn about the topic you were supposed to write about. But even worse, you undermine your self-respect by doing something that you know in your heart of hearts is wrong. That's too much of a price to pay for just a good grade.

three

HOW CAN YOU AVOID PLAGIARIZING?

If you know you've plagiarized, it's the moment you dread most. Your teacher hands back everyone's paper but yours, and she announces she wants a word with you after class. Your mind begins to race, trying out every possible excuse. There has to be some convincing reason for copying that paper you submitted.

Some students, however, are shocked when their teacher accuses them of plagiarism. In their eyes, their work is truly their own, and they've done nothing wrong. How can someone not know they plagiarized? Actually, it's fairly easy for this to happen. Many students don't fully understand what plagiarism is. Even more don't really know how to avoid it. Often, that's not entirely their fault. Teachers, even good ones, don't always explain what they expect from their students. It might not be fair, but if you don't want to find yourself accused of plagiarism, it's largely up to you to learn how not to do it.

Quoting from a Source

Unintentional plagiarists run into the most problems with research papers. The assignment of a research paper can be confusing. On one hand, you're told to find, read, and refer to reliable outside sources on your topic. On the other hand, you're supposed to include your own ideas so that the paper is "original." And on top of it all, you have to make it completely clear which words and ideas are yours and which came from your sources.

The easiest way of incorporating other people's words and ideas into your paper is by quoting them. A quotation is text you reproduce from a source word for word. A short quote of no more than a few sentences should be enclosed in quotation marks. A longer quote should be set off as a block of text. It should have a space above and below it and should be indented on both sides.

Quoting a source can seem easy, but there are some things you need to consider. First of all, choose quotations carefully. Quote a source only if the language of the quotation is particularly important or something you want to comment on.

A common mistake is to quote too much. Even if each quotation is fully cited, a paper that just strings a bunch of quotations together is flirting with plagiarism. It also suggests that you have nothing original to say about your topic.

speaker, cautions, "Keeping your Web application secure is an ongoing process—new classes of vulnerabilities are discovered with surprising frequency, and if you don't keep on top of them you could be in for a nasty surprise."

Gavin Bell, author of *Building Social Web Applications*, writes, "Security is hard to do well; most frameworks and tools are set up to make things easy to hook up and implement, with security left as an afterthought." He also notes that site security is "painstaking work." Nonetheless, Bell advises, "It would be wise to make sure that your entire development team has a good understanding of the current security threats that exist on the Web."

Companies, organizations, and government agencies are taking heed. That is why the services of Internet security experts are ever more in demand.

Sources don't always have to be cited in a footnote. Sometimes, it's OK just to mention the name of the author and source in the text itself, as in the highlighted passage.

Paraphrasing Others' Ideas

Another way of adding ideas from a source is paraphrasing. As mentioned before, paraphrasing means rewriting something in your own words. Here's what paraphrasing isn't: reproducing a sentence, a paragraph, or even a page or two from a source and changing only a word here or there. That's plagiarism and will likely lead to that difficult conversation with your teacher that you're trying to avoid.

A good paraphrase doesn't include any important words from the original. Yes, you can reuse "the" and "and," but just about

every other word is off limits. It is definitely never OK to reproduce a full sentence in a paraphrase. If you use even a few words
from the original source, always put them in quotation marks.

To make sure you don't accidentally use words from a source,
don't paraphrase right after reading your notes. Let a little time
pass. That way, you give yourself a chance to process the information, which will help you restate it in your own way.

The bad news about paraphrasing is that it's hard. It takes
practice to feel comfortable doing it. It can be frustrating, too,
when you compare your paraphrase to the original author's
language. Your words might sound clunky in comparison, but
remember that the author has probably been writing profession-
ally for many years, maybe for many decades. In time, you'll get
better at expressing ideas in your own words—but only if you
keep at it.

Taking Good Notes

Sometimes, students who know the rules of quoting and paraphrasing can still mess up. The problem is often bad note-taking
skills. For instance, let's say you take down a quote from a
source in your notes but forget to enclose the quotation in quotation marks. Days or weeks later, you may mistake the quoted
words in your notes for a paraphrase. Without realizing it, you
can easily and innocently insert someone else's words in your
paper, all the while thinking they are your own. This is especially true if you cut and paste material directly from Internet
sources into notes you keep on a computer file.

Clearly, you have to be very careful when you cut and paste text into your notes. Get in the habit of taking the time to place all direct quotations in quotation marks. If you're taking notes on your computer, you may want to distinguish quotations further by putting them in bold face or a bright color. To be extra sure you don't confuse quotations with paraphrases, consider keeping two separate files of notes on any Internet source—one for cut-and-paste quotes and one for notes that you've put in your own words.

Citing Quotations and Ideas

So you know how to quote and paraphrase. Now there's no way you'll ever accidentally plagiarize, right? Not necessarily. There's another very important part to giving your sources credit—citation. In a research paper, every time you incorporate a direct quotation or a unique idea from a source into your paper, you must cite that source, or you can be accused of plagiarism.

What sources do you have to cite? Just about every type you can imagine. Words or ideas can come from all sorts of sources in all sorts of media. For instance, citations may provide information about books, magazines, newspapers, songs, movies, letters, interviews, DVDs, Web pages, or blogs. Remember, too, that any illustrations or charts that you don't create yourself need citations.

There are some things you don't have to cite. They include your own ideas, thoughts, and opinions. Artwork you made or laboratory results from experiments you performed don't need citations. You also don't have to cite what's called common knowledge. These are ideas or facts you can safely assume your readers know or can easily find in many basic reference sources. For instance, if you write, "Breast cancer is a serious disease," you don't have to cite this because it's a commonly accepted truth. Similarly, if you write, "The American Civil War ended in 1865," no citation is needed because this is an undisputed fact anyone can find in an encyclopedia.

Maybe you have no idea whether you should cite something or not. There's an easy answer to that problem: go ahead and do it. If in doubt, always cite. Having too many citations is rarely a problem, and if it is, it's a minor mistake. But having too few citations is a big problem that can get you branded as a plagiarist.

Keep in mind that you need a citation for every idea or quotation you use from a source. Say you write a ten-page paper. You use ideas from one source on page one and on page six. Don't think it's enough to cite the source just on page one. You have to cite the source every time you use any material from it.

Citations and Bibliographies

Citing sources is important, but how do you do it? Well, that depends on your teacher and your school. There are various well-established systems of citing sources, each with their own citation formats. In some, you include information about your source in a footnote or an endnote. In others, you insert the

Bibliography

Bell, Gavin. *Building Social Networking Applications.*
Sebastopol, CA: O'Reilly Media, Inc., 2009.
Bender, David. "Data Breaches in the Cloud: Looks
Like Rain?" *New York Law Journal,* August 5,
2009. Retrieved January 2010 (http://www.law.
com/jsp/lawtechnologynews/PubArticleLTN.
jsp?id=1202432771872&Data_Breaches_in_the_Cloud_
Looks_Like_Rain).
Brenner, Bill. "10 Predictions for 2010: Kaminsky and
Weatherford." Threat Post: The Kaspersky Lab Security

A bibliography is more than a list of books. It offers information about all sources you've used, including newspaper and magazine articles, Web sites, DVDs, videotapes, blog entries, and podcasts.

information into the text itself within parentheses. Teachers usually make it clear what citation system you should use and provide you with examples to follow. But if they don't, you need to ask them how they want you to handle citations.

In each system, citing a book or a newspaper is fairly simple. But figuring out how to cite some other sources, especially those involving newer technologies (such as a podcast or a video blog), may be tough. Again, feel free to ask your teacher for help. Your school librarian may also be able to give you advice.

For nearly every research paper, you also have to list all your sources in a bibliography. A bibliography generally appears at the end of a paper. The information in each bibliography entry varies with the citation style used. But with each style, an entry is supposed to provide enough information that your readers can track down the source for themselves.

Compiling a bibliography can seem hard, especially if you start putting it together after you've finished your paper. It's much better to work on your bibliography in the note-taking stage. Compiling your bibliography while you take notes will not only save you time in the long run, but it will also help you make sure you don't accidentally leave off an important source.

How Many Sources?

So how many sources and citations should appear in a paper? In short, you need to consult enough sources to understand your topic, and you need a citation for every quotation you use and idea you borrow. Following those rules is often difficult, especially if you haven't written many papers. If in doubt, you can use these simple guidelines offered by writing expert Barry Gilmore in his book *Plagiarism: Why It Happens, How to Prevent It*. He suggests you should have one source and two citations for every page in your paper. In other words, if you write a five-page paper, try to use at least five sources and include at least ten citations.

One other thing to keep in mind is how information from your sources is distributed throughout your paper. Let's say you follow Gilmore's rule on a ten-page paper, but for the information on pages one through nine, all your citations refer to just one of your ten sources. You may not be accused of pla- giarism, but your teacher is likely to frown on your heavy reliance on a single source.

Checking Your Work

Your teachers have probably told you that you should always proofread papers before handing them in. This final check of your work helps you catch any misspellings or other errors that could bring down your grade. But, after you've finished proofreading, you might want to add a new last step—a pla- giarism check.

Take a look through your manuscript and ask yourself these questions. Do all the quotations have citations? Does every quo- tation match the source word for word? Do your paraphrases contain any important words from the original source? Are all the sources you've cited in your bibliography? Are your citations and bibliography entries in the proper format? Are they missing any information?

If you've used a lot of Internet sources and you're afraid you might have accidentally copied from them, think about going on a Google treasure hunt. Choose a few random phrases from your paper and enter them into a search engine. Obviously, if one of your sources pops up, you need to rework the phrase because it's too close to the original wording. To be extra careful, you might even want to swap papers with a friend so that each of you can

Before turning in a paper, get in the habit of doing a plagiarism check. Make sure you've cited every quotation, paraphrased quotations properly, and included all your sources in the bibliography.

check the other's work. If nothing comes up, you can be pretty sure that, at least where Internet sources are concerned, your work is plagiarism-free.

By now you probably know that avoiding plagiarism isn't all that easy. It requires some thought and some real hard work. After all, writing papers isn't a talent you're born with. It's something you learn to do, basically, by doing it. Furthermore, if you are going to college, research papers are likely to be a part of your life for years to come. If you figure out how to write them now, you'll save yourself from a lot of headaches in the future.

four

WHAT WILL HAPPEN IF YOU GET CAUGHT PLAGIARIZING?

In 1976, musician George Harrison was accused in court of reusing the melody of another song for his hit "My Sweet Lord." A court found him guilty of copyright infringement and ordered him to pay more than $1 million. A member of the Beatles, Harrison is now revered as one of the greatest rock stars of all time.

In 2002, popular historian Doris Kearns Goodwin was revealed to have plagiarized portions of her book *The Fitzgeralds and the Kennedys*. Goodwin kept a low profile for a while, but today she remains a best-selling author and frequent television talk-show guest.

In 1987, presidential candidate Joseph Biden was accused of stealing portions of a campaign speech from a British politician. The scandal forced him to drop out of

Former Beatle George Harrison was found guilty of copyright infringement in 1976 in a lawsuit involving his song "My Sweet Lord." Never admitting any wrongdoing, he wrote a tune called "This Song" that mocked the trial and the judgment.

the race. Twenty-one years later, Biden was elected vice president of the United States.

Based on these three stories, the consequences of plagiarism don't seem that serious. Of course, when they were first accused of plagiarism, Harrison, Goodwin, and Biden faced some initial embarrassment and loss of prominence in their chosen fields. But as time passed, the public no longer seemed to care that they had done something wrong. With their past plagiarism forgiven and largely forgotten, all three saw their reputations almost completely restored.

Punishments for Plagiarizing

If you're considering plagiarizing an assignment, those stories are probably encouraging. If even public figures can become even more famous and respected after being accused of plagiarism, what does a middle school or high school student have to worry about? Actually, as odd as it sounds, a student will often receive a harsher punishment for plagiarizing than someone in the public eye.

First of all, many schools have a policy of not tolerating any cheating, including plagiarism. Increasingly, schools ask students to sign an honor code, which states that the school expects students to do honest work. This document may lay out specific punishments that students can anticipate if they dare violate the code. Even if a school does not have a formal honor code, individual teachers may explain similar rules for students, either in writing or in conversation. However it's communicated to you, if your school or teacher has a specific policy about plagiarism, you had best take it seriously. If your instructors have taken the time to think about how to respond to plagiarism, they are very likely to enforce their rules.

What possible punishment do you face? In some cases, students caught plagiarizing may be kicked out of school, although expulsion is more common in colleges and universities than in high schools. More likely, a plagiarist will flunk the class or, at the very least, flunk the assignment.

If plagiarists are lucky, they may be given a chance to redo the assignment. But keep in mind, the teacher may automatically give the second try a worse grade than work of similar quality turned in by nonplagiarizing students. For example, a teacher may mark down an A-quality redo with a C as a punishment for plagiarizing. Even if that's not the school's or the teacher's official policy, an angry teacher may want to teach you a lesson.

Facing Your Accuser

No matter what policy a school has, if you are caught plagiarizing, you are going to face a fairly agonizing conversation. Your teacher is likely to take you aside and grill you on your work. If you can't answer your teacher's questions because you copied your work, expect to be embarrassed. But let's say you didn't mean to plagiarize. Maybe you didn't cite every idea you took from a source, or you paraphrased your sources badly. If your teacher accepts your defense, what you did was still technically plagiarism. Your teacher may be less angry with you than if you simply bought a paper. However, you are still in deep trouble.

If you get caught plagiarizing, you can expect to have an embarrassing and difficult conversation with your teacher. You'll likely also receive a formal punishment, such as a failing grade or even expulsion.

Keep in mind, too, that this awkward conversation may not be between just you and your teacher. The offense may be deemed serious enough to bring in your school principal or, even worse, your parents. Your mother and father may be the most easygoing people in the world. But if they have to make a special visit to your school to hear how their child is a plagiarizer, how do you think they are going to respond? If you are like most kids, you can expect a punishment at home as big, if not bigger, than the one you receive at school.

Think for a moment, too, about what a charge of plagiarism means. It suggests to others that you are fundamentally a dishonest person. Being labeled a plagiarist is likely to erode your relationship with your parents. If you were willing to lie to get a grade, they may ask themselves, what else are you lying about? Your teacher probably will assume that once a cheater, always a cheater, and she may be suspicious about any work you submit in the future. You can be sure, too, that if you are identified as a plagiarist, word will get around. Your other teachers will know, as will your fellow students. Many will start seeing you as a person not wholly worthy of their trust.

Policing Plagiarism

Even when students know they face harsh punishments for plagiarizing, many still do it. They assume that there's no way they'll get caught. But in reality, teachers are more likely now than ever before to pick up on plagiarizing. Just as the Internet has made it easier to plagiarize, it has also made it easier to catch plagiarists.

One new tool teachers have at their disposal is anti-plagiarism software. The most popular is available from Turnitin.com. For a fee, teachers can upload a student paper to this Web site. The Turnitin software will then compare it to its database of some forty million student papers and twelve billion Web pages. Turnitin returns the original paper with any potentially plagiarized passages marked in color.

Not all schools subscribe to a service like Turnitin. But keep in mind that any teacher can use a free antiplagiarism site (such as dustball.com/cs/plagiarism.checker) or even a search engine

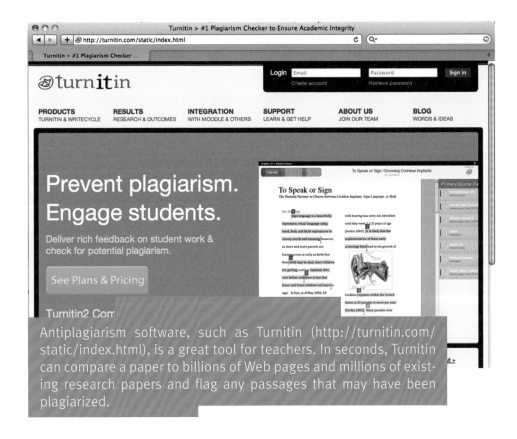

Antiplagiarism software, such as Turnitin (http://turnitin.com/static/index.html), is a great tool for teachers. In seconds, Turnitin can compare a paper to billions of Web pages and millions of existing research papers and flag any passages that may have been plagiarized.

such as Google or Yahoo! to look for the source of a suspicious passage. If you turn in a cut-and-paste job or buy a used paper online, a teacher with a talent for Internet searches can find concrete evidence of your plagiarism in a matter of seconds.

In recent years, there has been a rise in companies that sell custom research papers online. These paper mills promise to provide clients with original papers that won't be flagged by antiplagiarism software or a simple Internet search. Custom papers aren't cheap; many paper mills charge as much as $50 per page. Even at that price, the papers they produce are often of poor quality. These businesses may have an address in the United States, but they usually farm out work to writers with limited English skills in countries such as Nigeria and the Philippines. So in exchange for a small fortune, you may end up with an awful paper. You may be able to pass it off as your own work, but then again you probably won't want to.

Cheating Yourself

Although the odds are against it, there is always a chance you can get away with plagiarism. Maybe your teacher isn't paying attention or doesn't want the hassle of confronting you without absolute proof of what you've done. Maybe you just got lucky. If your plagiarizing goes undetected, it can seem like a pretty great deal. You got a good grade with almost no effort. What could be bad about that?

Well, you may have escaped punishment from your teacher, your school, and your parents, but you've still punished yourself. If you didn't do your own work, you didn't learn anything. If you wrote your own paper, even if it wasn't very good, you would have found out something about the topic. You probably would also become better at taking notes, citing sources, and creating a written argument. All those skills will likely come in handy in other high school courses. Plus, if you go on to college, you can expect your class workload to get much heavier. Don't you want to be ready? If you've relied on plagiarizing to get through your high school classes, you won't be prepared for college coursework.

Even if your teacher doesn't punish you for plagiarizing, you punish yourself when you don't do your own work. Only by finishing assignments on your own will you master a subject and learn to organize and communicate your ideas.

But there's another, better reason for doing your own work in high school: doing honest work is really the only way you can find out what subjects really excite you. Let's say your parents are English professors and want you to follow in their footsteps. Even though you resent them for telling you what to do with the rest of your life, you want to make a good grade in English to keep them off your back. You do a cut-and-paste job on a literary analysis on *The Scarlet Letter*, the classic American novel by Nathaniel Hawthorne. Somehow, with your after-school job and your other classes, you never got around to actually reading the book. Even so, you are a pretty skilled cutter and paster, so your teacher doesn't bat an eye. You even get a B+.

If you just wanted to make a good grade, you should be able to look back at what you've done and feel good. But you are missing the bigger picture. You might have fattened your grade point average but you did not learn much—not just about *The Scarlet Letter* but about yourself.

Let's say you actually did the assignment. You might have started reading *The Scarlet Letter* with little enthusiasm, assuming it was just the kind of dull book your parents were always trying to get you to read. But somewhere in the first few chapters, you got hooked. As soon as you reached the end, you got on the Internet to find articles about the book. You even checked a few books out of the library. You loved reading what other people said about the book, even if you didn't agree with a lot of it. By the time you finished taking notes, you had not only a good sense of scholarly opinions about the book but also why and how it had moved you. You get an A, and your teacher tells you it's the best paper he's read all year. Better yet, you show it to your parents and even they are impressed.

Let's imagine another scenario. Again, you decide to read *The Scarlet Letter* and research the paper without any help. But this time, a few pages into the novel, you are so bored you could die. But you keep reading, and after what seems like an eternity, you finish the book. You really hated it, but you go on the Internet and to the library and read a bunch of articles written by people who seemed to love it. You try to put together a coherent paper, even though your heart isn't in it. To your shock, you get a B, and your teacher tells you it was a good effort. But for you it was more than that—it was an education in what you don't want to study. Judging all of American and English literature from one book is probably a mistake. But still, it may not be too soon to prepare your mom and dad for the news that there is no way you are going to become an English teacher.

As this example shows, plagiarism robs you of important self-knowledge. You'll never discover whether you love or hate a subject unless you honestly attempt to learn about it. Who can say how you might feel about Franklin Delano Roosevelt's New Deal or about Edgar Degas's dancers or about Adam Smith's invisible hand? Chances are, none of those things means much, if anything, to you now. Well, then go ahead and look them up. Who knows, you might learn something. The subjects might bore you or leave you cold. Then again, they might ignite a new interest, one so big that you will want to spend your life pursuing it. You'll never know until you try.

Ten Great Questions to Ask Your Teacher

1 How do you define plagiarism?

2 How common is plagiarism in your classroom?

3 What are the most popular methods of plagiarizing?

4 Does the Internet make it easier to plagiarize and get away with it?

5 Can you plagiarize without realizing it?

6 What makes you suspect a paper is plagiarized?

7 If a student plagiarizes, what punishment can he or she expect?

8 Are some types of plagiarism considered worse than others?

9 How do students react when you accuse them of plagiarizing?

10 Why do students plagiarize?

HOW ARE ATTITUDES ABOUT PLAGIARISM CHANGING?

In January 2010, seventeen-year-old Helene Hegemann from Germany saw her novel *Axolotl Roadkill* published to great acclaim. An exploration of Berlin's club scene, the book was a hit with readers and critics and quickly landed on Germany's best-seller lists. Just as Hegemann was finding fame as a fresh literary voice, a blogger revealed that she had copied portions of her book from another novel. In one case, Hegemann had reproduced almost a full page of text with only a few word changes.

Helene Hegemann may remind you of Kaavya Viswanathan from chapter 1. Both teenage novelists were hailed in the media before they were revealed to be plagiarists. But the similarities between their stories end there. When Viswanathan's plagiarism was revealed, she immediately tried to

German teen Helene Hegemann made a splash with her book *Axolotl Roadkill*. When she was accused of plagiarizing portions of the novel, she offered no apology. Hegemann said borrowing from other works was all part of her creative process.

explain away her copying, claiming it was all an accident. Even so, she was publicly shamed for what she did, and her writing career was over. Hegemann, on the other hand, made no apology for her plagiarism. She was instead proud of incorporating another novelist's work into her own book. Hegemann said she was part of a creative movement that saw nothing wrong with borrowing from other works and mixing them together to create art. According to the *New York Times*, she claimed the world is now so saturated in media that "there's no such thing as originality anyway, just authenticity." The literary world did not turn its back on Hegemann. In fact, her book was nominated for a prestigious award *after* her plagiarism was revealed.

Creative Borrowing

Why did Hegemann's story play out so differently from Viswanathan's? Some variation in how Germans and Americans view plagiarism may have had a role, but most likely the difference was due to changing ideas introduced by new technologies. Computers and the Internet make it easy to share and reuse all sorts of materials, including text, music, video clips, and images. Especially for young people, it hardly seems unnatural to use technology to mix and match creative works to produce something new.

This attitude is often traced back to the practice of sampling melodies from other songs in hip-hop music. But, in truth, there has never been a time when creative people did not borrow from artists they admired. William Shakespeare based many of his plays on plots created by other writers. Pablo Picasso painted his own versions of famous works of art. T. S. Eliot, considered one of the greatest poets of the twentieth century, inserted many quotations (without quotation marks) in his famous poem "The Waste Land." In an essay about the seventeenth-century English dramatist Philip Massinger, Eliot once stated, "Immature poets imitate; mature poets steal; bad poets deface what they take, and good poets make it into something better, or at least something different."

Many of today's writers would agree with Eliot. Among them is David Shields. His book *Reality Hunger,* which was compiled in large part from quotations from other works, challenges conventional ideas about plagiarism and suggests that freely borrowing from other works could breathe new life into modern literature. Another writer exploring similar ideas is Jonathan Lethem, author of the novels *Motherless Brooklyn* and *The Fortress of Solitude.* Lethem set out his defense of artists borrowing from other artists in his 2007 essay "The Ecstasy of Influence: A Plagiarism," which, like Shields's book, unabashedly includes unmarked quotations and borrowed ideas. Lethem has also established the Promiscuous Materials Project. As explained on his Web site, through this project he invites filmmakers and playwrights to adapt some of his short stories. Normally, they would have to pay a fee for the dramatic rights to Lethem's work, but he charges them only $1 for each story used. As Lethem explains, "As I researched ["The Ecstasy of Influence"] I came

American novelist and short story writer Jonathan Lethem charges filmmakers and playwrights just $1 for the right to adapt some of his stories. This experiment emerged from his belief that artists should have more freedom to reuse and recast art made by other people.

more and more to believe that artists should ideally find ways to make material free and available for reuse. This project is a (first) attempt to make my own art practice reflect that belief."

Lethem was influenced by the free culture movement. Advocates of free culture think that copyright laws are too constraining. They want to see more creative works available for free on the Internet for people to use or reuse however they see fit. An important part of this movement is Creative Commons. Through its Web site, this organization provides free licenses for works that let their creators reserve some rights, while, under

Through its Web site (http://freeculture.org), Students for Free Culture brings together college students interested in allowing more public access to digital information and in making copyright laws less restrictive.

many conditions, allowing others to use their works without asking for permission or paying a fee. Millions of works, including artwork, songs, and videos, are now available under Creative Commons licenses. Also looking to change ideas about copyright and intellectual property is Students for Free Culture. Founded in 2003, this group has more than forty chapters in colleges and universities in the United States and abroad.

The Uses of Plagiarism

Conventional notions about plagiarism are also being challenged by Rebecca Moore Howard, a professor of writing and rhetoric at Syracuse University. Moore Howard suggests that what most teachers would consider plagiarism is actually a helpful learning tool. For instance, she holds that copying from a text and changing a few words or the structure of a few sentences can help students see how good writing works. Art students are often instructed to copy great paintings so that they can understand them better. Moore Howard believes that writing students could similarly benefit by learning through imitation.

In an editorial published in 2007 in the *Washington Post*, Jason Johnson, an information technology consultant, also made a case for allowing students to cut and paste. Titled "Cut-and-Paste Is a Skill, Too," he declared that the "term paper is dead," killed by "the rise of the Internet and its endless bounty." Johnson argued that teachers should stop spending so much time acting as the plagiarism police. He advised them instead to give up the research paper and start making assignments that

A teacher and her students view artwork in a gallery. The wealth of information available for free on the Internet is encouraging students and teachers to discuss the case for and against reusing old materials to create something new.

take better advantage of the rich sources of information available in the Internet age.

Not surprisingly, Johnson's editorial drew a wide range of comments. Some readers wrote the *Post* praising Johnson's innovative thinking; others deplored his efforts to let student plagiarists off the hook. As the response shows, the latest debates about whether it's right or wrong to borrow from other people's works is far from settled. By all means, explore these new ideas. Talk about them with your friends, and bring them up in class. But for the time being, it's smart to do everything you can to avoid what your teachers still call plagiarism. Maybe in the future, that definition will change. For now, though, you need to do your own work or face the consequences.

Glossary

bibliography List of books, Web sites, and other sources consulted while writing a research paper or similar work.

citation Listing that identifies the title and other basic information about the source of an idea or a quotation.

common knowledge Facts and ideas that one can expect most people to know.

copyright Legally recognized ownership of a creative work, such as a book, painting, or song.

copyright infringement Illegal use of copyrighted material without the consent of the copyright holder.

Creative Commons Nonprofit organization that grants licenses to creative works that give others limited rights to use the works without the permission of the creator.

cryptomnesia Mental process in which people unconsciously recall words or ideas of another person and mistakenly believe they created the words or ideas themselves.

cut and paste Process of using a computer program to copy text directly from one document into another.

fair use Legal doctrine that allows for the use of a small portion of a copyrighted work without the permission of the copyright holder.

honor code Set of rules established by a school or classroom regarding issues of plagiarism and cheating.

intellectual property Creative work or invention for which the creator may claim legal recognition of ownership, such as a copyright, trademark, or patent.

paper mill Business that sells existing or custom-made research papers to students, which they then usually represent as their own work.

paraphrasing Explaining the ideas expressed in the work of another writer in one's own words.

plagiarism Practice of presenting another person's works or ideas as one's own.

public domain Work that is not protected by copyright and therefore legally can be reprinted or reproduced by any member of the public.

quotation Reproduction of a portion of a text word for word.

research paper Work, usually written for a classroom assignment, that combines ideas taken from other sources with the author's own ideas about a topic.

self-plagiarizing Submitting the same paper or written assignment in more than one class without the permission of the instructors.

Turnitin.com Web-based company whose software compares a submitted paper to Web sites and other available papers and identifies passages that were possibly plagiarized.

Center for Academic Integrity (CAI)
126 Hardin Hall
Clemson University
Clemson, SC 29634
(864) 656-1293
Web site: http://www.academicintegrity.org
The CAI brings together more than 350 high schools and
   colleges to share ideas about policies to promote academic integrity among their students.

Center for Intellectual Property
University of Maryland University College
Largo Academic Center, Room 2405
3501 University Boulevard East
Adelphi, MD 20783
(240) 684-2803
Web site: http://www.umuc.edu/distance/odell/
   cip/mission.shtml
This organization explores issues involving plagiarism,
   copyright, and academic honesty in American colleges
   and universities.

Chapman Learning Commons
Room 300, Irving K. Barber Learning Centre

University of British Columbia

1961 East Mall

Vancouver, BC V6T 1Z1

Canada

(604) 827-3909

Web site: http://clc.library.ubc.ca/airc.html

On its Web site, this center presents an interactive tutorial
for students about what plagiarism is and how to
avoid it.

Creative Commons

171 Second Street, Suite 300

San Francisco, CA 94105

(415) 369-8480

Web site: http://creativecommons.org

Creative Commons provides licenses that allow the public to
use creative works freely under some conditions without
endangering the works' copyright protection.

National Writing Project

University of California

2105 Bancroft Way, #1042

Berkeley, CA 94720

(510) 642-0963

Web site: http://www.nwp.org

Through a network of local Web sites and organizations, the
National Writing Project promotes the teaching of writing in
American schools.

U.S. Copyright Office
James Madison Memorial Building
101 Independence Avenue SE
Washington, DC 20540
(202) 707-3000
Web site: http://www.copyright.gov
The U.S. Copyright Office offers information about how and
    why copyrights are issued for creative works.

Web Sites

Due to the changing nature of Internet links, Rosen Publishing
has developed an online list of Web sites related to the subject
of this book. This site is updated regularly. Please use this link
to access the list:

http://www.rosenlinks.com/faq/plag

For Further Reading

Chin, Beverly. *How to Write a Great Research Paper*. San Francisco, CA: Jossey-Bass, 2004.

Engdahl, Sylvia. *Intellectual Property Rights*. Farmington Hills, MI: Greenhaven Press, 2009.

Espejo, Roman. *Copyright Infringement: Opposing Viewpoints*. Farmington Hills, MI: Greenhaven Press, 2009.

Francis, Barbara. *Other People's Words: What Plagiarism Is and How to Avoid It*. Berkeley Heights, NJ: Enslow Publishers, 2005.

Gaines, Ann. *Don't Steal Copyrighted Stuff! Avoiding Plagiarism and Illegal Internet Downloading*. Berkeley Heights, NJ: Enslow Publishers, 2007.

Gilmore, Barry. *Plagiarism: A How-Not-to Guide for Students*. Portsmouth, NH: Heinemann, 2009.

Kesselman-Turkel, Judi, and Franklynn Peterson. *Note-Taking Made Easy*. Madison, WI: University of Wisconsin Press, 2003.

Kesselman-Turkel, Judi, and Franklynn Peterson. *Secrets to Writing Great Papers*. Madison, WI: University of Wisconsin Press, 2003.

Munger, David, and Shireen Campbell. *What Every Student Should Know About Researching Online*. New York, NY: Longman, 2006.

Stern, Linda. *What Every Student Should Know About Avoiding Plagiarism*. New York, NY: Longman, 2006.

Blum, Susan D. *My Word! Plagiarism and College Culture.* Ithaca, NY: Cornell University Press, 2009.

Demirjian, Karoun. "What Is the Price of Plagiarism?" *Christian Science Monitor*, May 11, 2006. Retrieved March 28, 2010 (http://www.csmonitor.com/2006/0511/p14s01-lire.html).

Eisner, Caroline, and Martha Vicinus, eds. *Originality, Imitation, and Plagiarism: Teaching Writing in the Digital Age.* Ann Arbor, MI: University of Michigan Press, 2008.

Gilmore, Barry. *Plagiarism: Why It Happens, How to Prevent It.* Portsmouth, NH: Heinemann, 2008.

Gladwell, Malcolm. "Something Borrowed." Gladwell.com, November 22, 2004. Retrieved March 31, 2010 (http://www.gladwell.com/2004/2004_11_25_a_borrowed.html).

Hansen, Brian. "Combating Plagiarism." *CQ Researcher*, September 19, 2003. Retrieved March 26, 2010 (http://www.cqpress.com/docs/Combating%20Plagiarism.pdf).

Johnson, Jason. "Cut-and-Paste Is a Skill, Too." *Washington Post*, March 25, 2007. Retrieved April 6, 2010 (http://www.washingtonpost.com/wp-dyn/content/article/2007/03/23/AR2007032301612.html).

Juskalian, Russ. "You Didn't Plagiarize, Your Unconscious Did." *Newsweek*, July 7, 2009. Retrieved April 1, 2010 (http://www.newsweek.com/id/205560).

Kennedy, Randy. "The Free-Appropriation Writer." *New York Times*, February 26, 2010. Retrieved March 10, 2010 (http://www.nytimes.com/2010/02/28/weekinreview/28kennedy.html?ref=europe).

Kulish, Nicholas. "Author, 17, Says It's 'Mixing,' Not Plagiarism." *New York Times*, February 11, 2010. Retrieved March 10, 2010 (http://www.nytimes.com/2010/02/12/world/europe/12germany.html?hp).

Lethem, Jonathan. "The Ecstasy of Influence: A Plagiarism." *Harper's Magazine*, February 2007. Retrieved April 2, 2010 (http://www.harpers.org/archive/2007/02/0081387).

Lipson, Charles. *Doing Honest Work in College*. 2nd ed. Chicago, IL: University of Chicago Press, 2008.

Mallon, Thomas. *Stolen Words: The Classic Book on Plagiarism*. Updated ed. San Diego, CA: Harcourt, 2001.

National Public Radio. "Cut and Paste Plagiarism." *Talk of the Nation*, February 14, 2006.

Posner, Richard A. *The Little Book of Plagiarism*. New York, NY: Pantheon Books, 2007.

Roberts, Tim, ed. *Student Plagiarism in an Online World*. Hershey, PA: Information Science Reference, 2008.

Index

About the Author

Liz Sonneborn is a writer who lives in Brooklyn, New York. A graduate of Swarthmore College, she is the author of more than eighty books for children, young adults, and adult readers. She has also written a guide to English grammar, style, and usage for a leading software company.

Photo Credits

Cover © www.istockphoto.com/Richard Bowden; p. 5 Daniel Acker/Bloomberg via Getty Images; pp. 10, 15, 41 Shutterstock; p. 18 Courtesy of Cleveland Heights High School Library; pp. 20–21 © Mark Richards/PhotoEdit; p. 31 © Cleve Bryant/PhotoEdit; p. 34 Richard E. Aaron/Redferns/Getty Images; p. 37 DK Stock/Christina Kennedy/Getty Images; p. 39 iParagrams, LLC; p. 46 Jens Schlueter/AFP/Getty Images; pp. 48–49 Valerio Pennicino/Getty Images; p. 50 Students for Free Culture; p. 52 Comstock/Thinkstock.

Designer: Evelyn Horowicz; Editor: Kathy Kuhtz Campbell; Photo Researcher: Marty Levick